j915.1 Tang, Yungmei
TAN
        China, here we
        come!

9.95

j915.1 Tang, Yungmei
TAN
        China, here we
        come!

DATE	BORROWER'S NAME	
MAR 10	████████████	
APR 2 3	██████████████	
APR 1 6 1987		

CHINA, HERE WE COME!

CHINA, HERE WE COME!

Visiting the People's Republic of China

TANG YUNGMEI

G. P. PUTNAM'S SONS
New York

For Karen
and her friends in America and China

and for Han Suyin

Map on page 8 by Edward L. Miliano

NOTE:

The spelling of Chinese place names and references
follows the official transliteration system *(Hanyu pinyin)*
of the People's Republic of China. Old-style names of the
major cities are given in parentheses.

Book design by Kathleen Westray
Library of Congress Cataloging in Publication Data
Tang, Yungmei.
China, here we come!
Summary: Describes China today as seen through the
eyes of a group of American high school students.
1. China—Description and travel—1976–
2. Tang, Yungmei. [1. China—Description and travel]
I. Title.
DS712.T36   915.1'0458   81-12174
ISBN 0-399-20826-7   AACR2
Second Impression

CONTENTS

GOING TO CHINA
(7)

ON OUR WAY
(9)

BEIJING
(11)

NANJING
(25)

HANGZHOU
(33)

SHANGHAI
(45)

OUR LAST DAY
(59)

MEMORIES
(61)

(6)

GOING TO China for us thirteen-year-olds was overwhelming. We had never thought of taking such a long trip. We didn't know much about China. We knew it was very old and a socialist country, and we had seen pictures of the Great Wall.

We had six months to prepare for the trip, and we wanted to learn as much as we could. Yungmei arranged for all of us to meet once a week after school. We saw documentaries and slides on different aspects of Chinese life: the role of women, childcare, education, and the use of acupuncture in surgery. We watched historic films on the early dynasties and found out that the Chinese invented the compass, papermaking and gunpowder. We had discussions with people who had spent time in China: writers and filmmakers, and also a farmer from Pennsylvania who told us about life on a commune. We read about old customs as well as life today. We spent long hours studying the map of China, and we went to museums to see Chinese art collections. Together we prepared Chinese dishes and had delicious Cantonese meals in Chinatown.

Each of us worked hard to prepare a song and dance show for the Chinese children we would meet. We even learned a Chinese song, and we brought many small presents to give them: skateboards, yo-yos, kaleido-scopes and picture books.

Our parents made contributions for the trip, but we also raised money on our own by selling raffle tickets and posters, babysitting, and walking dogs.

We would be the youngest group of Americans to visit China since it became socialist. We couldn't wait to go. We wanted to see for ourselves a school and a commune. We wanted to stand on the Great Wall. Each of us planned to keep an individual diary to write about the places we would see and the people we would meet.

THE 1979 CHINA STUDY PROJECT

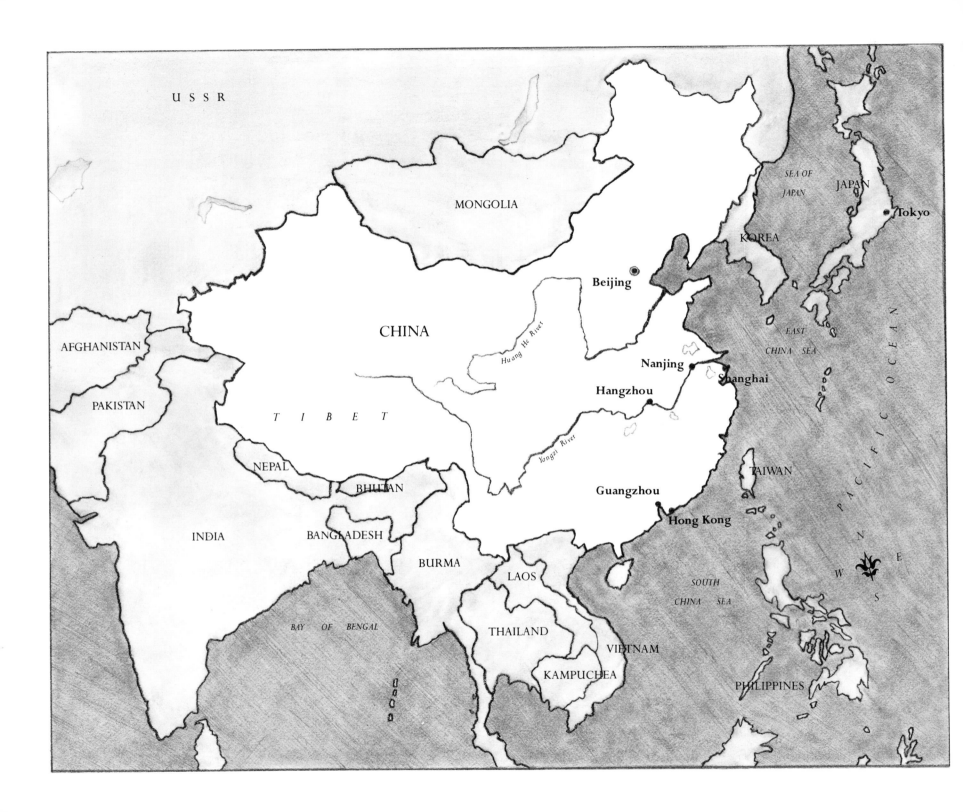

WE ARE on a plane going to China and we still can't believe it! But it's true. We will be in China for almost three weeks visiting four major cities: the capital, Beijing (Peking), Nanjing (Nanking), Hangzhou (Hankow), and Shanghai. We'll also stay a day in Guangzhou (Canton) before leaving for Hong Kong and returning home to New York.

The first part of the journey is from New York to Tokyo and it takes fifteen hours, with a one-hour stopover for fuel in Anchorage, Alaska. We go from one time zone to another, which means that while we are sleeping on the plane, our friends in New York are doing their homework after a day in school. We even jump a whole day ahead of ourselves: While we are watching the sun setting in Tokyo, the sun is rising in New York.

We leave Tokyo at 3:15 in the afternoon on Monday, May 7, on China Airlines. We are on the way to Beijing. New York to Beijing: almost 8,059 miles in just over twenty hours' flying time. We can hardly believe we are halfway around the world. But when we see the Chinese dressed in their blue, gray or green tunics and wearing "Chinese slippers," it all begins to seem real.

Now we are in China! We dreamed of it so much. A country with a recorded history dating back four thousand years. An immense land about the same size as America, with over 900 million people.

(10)

BEIJING (PEKING) IS both the political and cultural capital of China. It was here on October 1, 1949, that Mao Zedong proclaimed the founding of the People's Republic of China, and became the leader of the socialist government. Beijing has modern administrative buildings and a new subway which runs straight through the city. There are historical and archeological museums, the Peking Opera house, old and new hotels, many theaters and sports stadiums. The old Imperial Palace of the dynastic emperors has been preserved.

The city is spread over 6,780 square miles and is the second most populated city in China, with almost 8 million people.

ON OUR first morning in Beijing as we drive through the city on our way to the Kang Le Li Primary School we see an endless flow of people on black bicycles. The sun is shining in a faint haze through the green leaves of trees lining the roadside. Our bus honks its way through the cyclists.

At the school we are introduced to some of the staff and they tell us how the school works. There are eight hundred students, with eighty teachers and staff members. Each teacher has thirty to forty children in a class. Beginning from age seven, every child in China is required to go to school six days a week, from 8:00 in the morning until 4:00 in the afternoon, with a two-hour break for lunch and recreation.

We go to a first-grade classroom where students are learning multiplication with panda pictures stuck on a blackboard. Children wear multicolored shirts and pants, and many of them have red scarves around their necks. Almost all of the boys have short haircuts; the girls have many different styles, some short and some long in braids. A staff member tells us that those with red scarves are members of the Communist Youth League.

(12)

We are struck by the self-discipline of the children. They are at their desks all in rows silently facing the teacher with their hands behind their backs until he asks a question of the whole class. They then chant an answer in unison. The teacher asks individual students to answer next, and all of them quickly raise their hands, keeping their elbows on their desks with palms facing inward.

In a second-grade class, children are learning how to write characters. First, the teacher writes a character on the blackboard, slowly, stroke by stroke. Then a volunteer comes up to copy the strokes.

As we enter a fourth-grade natural science class (what the Chinese call "common knowledge"), all the students clap in welcome. Jars filled with various roots are laid out on tables. At each table, five children pass around a magnifying glass to study the roots. "Plants are a symbol of friendship, like our relations with our American friends," the

teacher says. "If the roots are deep and strong, leaves will develop and flowers of friendship will bloom."

In a music class, children holding red banners and standing at attention are singing a military song under the watchful eyes of Chairman Hua Guofeng, China's present leader, and Mao Zedong, who look down at them from photographs on the wall.

In a fifth-grade English language class, the teacher points to flashcards with pictures and written phrases, and asks his students to repeat the phrases in English. After a while he interrupts the lesson and leads them in a welcoming song sung in English to the tune of "Clementine."

As they finish singing, a bell rings and the children start rubbing their temples, the bridges of their noses and their foreheads while a voice over a loudspeaker gives directions. It looks strange to us, but we are told this is the daily five-minute eye exercise to develop good eyesight that is repeated morning and afternoon in every school.

When the exercise is over, we and the whole student body go out into the courtyard for a ten-minute recess. The children play games, chase each other, jump or throw balls. Some practice Taiji Quan, a form of shadow boxing known in the West as Tai Chi.

Inside, everyone was so quiet and attentive. Now they are noisy and exuberant. As soon as the bell rings again, all stop, and quickly line up in rows covering the entire courtyard. There is no pushing, shoving or talking.

Following the movements of a gym teacher, they begin their morning calisthenics and to our amazement do them in perfect unison. Some of us try to copy them, but we stand out like sore thumbs.

Now we all march into an auditorium where we will do the show we rehearsed in New York. We will perform for the Chinese children and they for us. We are all a little nervous about being on stage for the first time.

We start by singing "The Star-Spangled Banner." Then Ellen does a gymnastics solo and Zack performs his magic trick. He sticks a needle into a balloon and it doesn't burst. John does a juggling act with tennis balls. Our hosts are very enthusiastic as they laugh and clap. Now it is their turn. They sing and do dances inspired by Chinese daily life on communes, in factories and schools. It's so perfect, we are mesmerized.

We have a great time when they try to dance a Virginia reel with us. Everyone has lots of fun matching steps.

Then together we sing *"Wo Ai Beijing Tian An Men"* in Chinese and in English. This means "I love Beijing's Gate of Heavenly Peace," and it is a popular song sung by children all over China. While we are all singing, six exquisite little girls step forward and do a ballet sequence.

When it is over, we all go back to the courtyard. Danny is on his skateboard, showing our hosts how to use it. Peggy hands out "I Love New York" buttons and Nat flies frisbees.

Nadia finds the teachers very encouraging and the children cooperative and well-behaved: "Kids don't look bored, although they sit with their hands behind their backs, very erect and serious."

We feel so happy to be here, and Michael sums it up for all of us when he says, "If this were all there was to our China trip, I'd be satisfied to go home today."

WE ARE off to see the Imperial Palace, or Forbidden City, as it is often called (in the days of the emperors it was considered a capital offense for a common citizen or a foreigner to enter these grounds). Now it is a public museum with the old Imperial Gardens open to everyone.

The palace itself is fantastic and huge. Built during the Ming Dynasty (A.D. 1368–1644), it has over 9,000 rooms and fifteen layers of stone underground which prevented anyone from tunneling their way in. A wide moat and a wall all around the grounds also kept people out.

All the buildings are red with yellow glazed roofs. The names of the palaces are beautiful: Palace of

Earthly Tranquility, Palace of Heavenly Purity, Hall of Supreme Harmony, Hall for the Preservation of Harmony, Hall of Mental Cultivation.

The palace rooms are full of gold carvings, large brass bowls, armor made out of thousands of pearls, and other sumptuous objects. We see bronze lions and turtles; gold knives, chopsticks, silver cooking utensils; incense burners; a golden throne; and a gigantic jade carving eight feet tall showing a landscape with mountains, trees, houses, people working and children playing.

As we wander through the buildings and grounds, we move among large crowds of visitors—most of them in families. The Chinese children are chewing large bread buns and licking popsicles. It is very hot and we also start licking chocolate, vanilla and red bean popsicles.

(18)

ANOTHER DAY we have lunch at the Summer Palace, which is northwest of Beijing on the shores of Kunming Lake. There are several palaces in the vicinity: one of them, the Garden of Golden Waves, was built in the twelfth century. The Ming and Qing emperors added pavilions, pagodas, gazebos, and a long covered passageway along the shore of the lake, called the "Painted Gallery," where we see paintings of historical and mythical scenes and landscapes of the city of Hangzhou. After lunch we go to look at the famous "Marble Boat." It is a houseboat with a marble base sitting in the lake and was built in the late 1800s by the Empress Dowager Ci Xi.

After touring the gardens and palaces, we take a short drive to the site where thirteen Ming emperors are buried. The Sacred Way leads to the tombs and is lined with twelve huge stone statues of animals and warriors dating from the fifteenth century. Camels, elephants, horses, lions, a *ji lin* (Chinese unicorn), literary figures in robes and warriors in uniform—all stand 10 to 15 feet tall. They are extraordinary. We are all so excited that none of us can resist climbing to the top of one animal or another.

(20)

THE GREAT WALL of China! From the train window we can see bits and pieces of the wall taunting us, slinking in and out of the mountains, which are magnificent in

themselves. They shoot up out of the ground, huge and sharp. This is the most spectacular Chinese scenery we will ever see.

To some of us, the Great Wall is more impressive than we thought it would be. It is hard to imagine that the wall is the only man-made object on earth that can be seen from the moon. It goes up and down the mountains, straight up and all the way around and down again, like a long snake, going around and around, with the tail coming back on itself.

The construction of the Great Wall was started by small kingdoms during the Spring and Autumn Era (770–476 B.C.) for protection against each other and holding back nomadic invasions from the north. In the Qin Dynasty period (221–206 B.C.) the emperor linked all the sections together, creating the 3,600-mile Great Wall that stands today.

Wide enough for five horsemen to ride side by side, the wall was used as a road: emperors moved men and equipment through the mountains. For centuries, it has protected central China.

The section we visit in the Badaling Pass, restored in 1957 for visitors, is 26 feet high on the average, 22 feet wide at the bottom and 19 feet wide on the top. There are battlements for observation and firing; guard towers for sentry posts; living quarters for soldiers; and beacon towers for communication and signaling.

Every step of the hike up the Great Wall is worth it. Ellen does one cartwheel and two walkovers just "for the record." John juggles on it with his tennis balls. Some of us walk up to a high tower but Ralph runs most of the way, racing Peggy and Jamie, and exhausts himself.

At the very top, the wall looks endless and the panorama is breathtaking. Crowds of Chinese visitors and foreign tourists are all over the wall. We shall always remember the Great Wall of China as big and steep, old and crumbly—and tiring!

(24)

NANJING

ON the plane flying south from Beijing to Nanjing (Nanking) we fly low enough to see terraces of lush green paddy fields stretched beneath us. Now we can see Nanjing lying on the south bank of the Yangzi River and surrounded by the Purple Mountains. It is an ancient city, built over 2,400 years ago, and was China's capital several times throughout history. Today it occupies 301 square miles, with almost 2.5 million people. Nanjing is very green: deep rows of trees line wide streets, and there is a beautiful lake with islands and pagodas.

The Nanjing Bridge which spans the Yangzi River is one of the most remarkable modern sights in the country. It connects north and south China. It took eight years to build with 7,000 people working every day, and was completed in 1968. It is 1,171 feet long and has two levels, a roadway on the upper level and a dual-track railway on the lower level. The stone foundation pillars look like the size of a basketball court. From a bridgehead at one end we can see the muddy swirling water, the dark green mountains and light green rice fields creeping up close to the river edge.

WE spend a whole day at the Nanjing Municipal School of Foreign Languages, a specialized school teaching English, French, German and Japanese in addition to basic subjects. We are the first foreign group to visit this school.

There are seventeen elementary and junior high classes, with a total of 680 students. The principal talks about the students: "They work hard to build China into a powerful socialist country. They are taught to be 'Red and Expert.' The students love their country and the socialist system. They have one common ideal—to bring about the Four Modernizations in industry, agriculture, science and technology, and defense."

A library with about 40,000 books in various languages has reading rooms for both teachers and students. Movies and tape recorders are among the audio-visual equipment used for language laboratory work.

We join in an English lesson with a class of sixteen-year-olds. There are microphones on every desk to speak into and listen from. The lesson is on "oral expression." The teacher treats us like her students. She questions us about the text they are reading aloud, and invites us to read passages too. We in turn ask questions of the students. We really feel we are a part of the class.

After class we break up into small groups to talk about each other's life-styles. Ellen is showing photographs of her family, her home, and talking about life in New York. Ralph shows his group how to play "dots" and "tic-tac-toe." A pretty young girl in a pink blouse asks Zack the difference between "beautiful" and "pretty." He finds it awkward to explain, and finally gives up, saying, "Beautiful is more pretty than pretty." Monica is explaining how she studies English grammar. A seventeen-year-old girl approaches Nadia, who is sitting by herself. "Would you like to be friends?" She takes Nadia's hand and they talk about writing to each other. Jamie is telling his group about what books he reads. The students also want to know if there are any tips he can give them on how to speak better English.

One of the girls wants to know what Michael's parents do and he answers, "Well, my father works for the government." The girl doesn't understand the English word "government." When Michael explains, she is puzzled. "Oh, but in my country everyone works for the government."

Others ask: "Do you have brothers and sisters?" "What do you do on Sundays?" "What classes do you have in school?" "How do you learn foreign languages?" "What is the best way to memorize English words?" But the most popular question is: "Do all young people in America watch a lot of television, and do they go to the movies every day?"

Some have seen Charlie Chaplin's movie, *Modern Times*, and a new American film, *Future World*. Others have read *David Copperfield*. They talk about English writers and we are surprised that our hosts know of Jack London, Charles Dickens, and

(28)

Mark Twain. And they also know a few English songs: "Auld Lang Syne," "Do-re-mi," and "We Shall Not Be Moved." We find it very easy to communicate with the Chinese.

In the afternoon we all perform as we did at the Kang Le Li Primary School in Beijing. A Chinese boy plays doctor in a skit on how to stay healthy. Two children with a toy animal complain that it won't go to sleep. The doctor says it's because its eyes are dirty and must be cleaned.

When their skit is finished, they take us to their recreation rooms. We play together, trying to toss a rubber ring over standup cardboard animals, all made and painted by the students. Rachel keeps missing. None of the Chinese laugh at her or tell her to give up. Instead, they insist, "Keep trying. You know, have fun. It's to have fun!" After trying and trying and never getting the ring over the target, Rachel stops and is given a prize for trying so hard.

ANOTHER DAY we go to visit the Nanjing Opera School with our friends from the Nanjing Municipal School of Foreign Languages.

On our way in the bus Karen makes close friends with a couple of girls, exchanging addresses, trying to give them tips on practicing English and talking a little French with one of them.

When we arrive the principal explains how the school is run. It is another specialized school subsidized by the government. Students are enrolled from a regular elementary school after examination, and they live at the school, receiving free tuition, food and medical care.

There are 600 boys and girls ranging in age from ten to twenty-three. Besides basic subjects, they learn different opera styles as well as traditional Peking opera, singing and dancing and stage arts. When they reach twelve they start to study martial arts, and at age seventeen they also study directing and playwriting. After graduation, at age twenty-three, they are sent by the school to provincial theaters.

(31)

(32)

WE ARE on a train bound for Hangzhou (Hankow), the city of tea and silk where Marco Polo settled in the thirteenth century when China was called "Cathay." Between the eighth and twelfth centuries Hangzhou was several times the capital of kingdoms and dynasties. In those days it was called Kinsai, "City of Heaven," and people traveled by boat, through streams and canals under hundreds of small bridges.

Up to 1949 there were only a few small factories and one textile mill. Since then the city has virtually been rebuilt, and new apartment buildings overshadow old single-story crowded houses. Today, Hangzhou has a population of 980,000 spread out over 165.6 square miles.

WE MAKE a short visit to the largest silk factory in China, where we see men and women in different sections of the factory reeling, weaving, dyeing and printing the silk. We see yards and yards of colorful silks and brocades that are exported all over the world. The factory has living quarters and facilities for the workers: dormitories for single people, apartments for families, a hospital, a library, a school, sports fields and a gymnasium.

ONE afternoon we go to the Hangzhou zoo, which was built only five years ago. It is a beautiful hilly wooded area with lovely traditionally designed houses for the animals. We see many strange animals we have never seen before, as well as the famous Chinese black and white pandas and the small golden lesser pandas. We stay a long time photographing them at play.

On another afternoon we take off on our own without our guides, and walk around town. As usual the Chinese look at us with friendliness and curiosity. Old people are happy to stop and say hello, and children follow us chatting and laughing.

On the sidewalks people are preparing food: chopping up turtle for soup, cleaning pigs, plucking chicken feet. Others are squatting on the curbs washing dishes and clothes.

We buy Chinese caps, some blue and some green, and the famous Hangzhou "Dragon Well" light green tea. Ralph buys a freshly steamed pork bun from a street stand. To pay for it, he has to first give the vendor money for a coupon and then give the coupon back.

As we wander through the streets, we see the old part of the city with its rows of cramped one-room homes made of wood and mud. We notice for the first time that some people here are wearing patched clothes. Through open doors we see the minimum of furniture: bed, table and chairs, but all the rooms are neat and clean.

When we continue on to the modern part of the city we see a real change—a lot of new brick buildings. It is largely residential, and the streets are not so crowded.

We stroll again in busy neighborhoods for the rest of the afternoon. This is what we like best of all: observing life in the streets.

(37)

ON OUR LAST day in Hangzhou we make our first visit to a commune, the Plum Blossom Tea Brigade of the West Lake People's Commune. It is a large tea plantation established five hundred years ago and owned by rich landlords until 1949.

Thirteen hundred people, making up two hundred and fifty households, live on 185.25 acres of tea garden and 1,976 acres of wooded hills and paddy fields.

In 1949, the output of tea was 401 pounds per acre. By 1978, tea production had reached 1,915 pounds per acre. The Tea Brigade has produced enough revenue over the years to buy tea-drying machines, electric ovens, trucks, tractors and cable hoists.

(40)

(41)

Members of the Brigade can own small private plots of land around their homes on which to grow crops and raise chickens, goats and pigs. They own their houses as well, and they cut firewood from trees on the mountains.

As in the silk factory we visited, there are many facilities for commune members: a nursery school and a kindergarten, a primary school and a middle school, a clinic with cooperative medical services for all the workers.

To organize and run the commune, workers elect a committee called the People's Congress. Workers do not receive wages. They are paid in part with food, clothing and housing, and in part with work points based on the quality and quantity of their production. Work points are converted into money, which each person can use as he or she wishes.

A family on a commune lives with all immediate relatives in one house. At dawn grandmother or mother goes out to get firewood to cook breakfast. By 6:30 or 7:00 A.M. everyone is off to work: parents to pick tea; grandmother to help with children at the nursery; and grandfather to cultivate the family's private plot of land. A child not yet in school might help in the Brigade's office or in the tea drying house. Communes do not have upper schools, so older students go to classes in a nearby urban district. When upper school is completed, a student can take a university entrance exam if he or she wishes. If a student does not go on to university, he or she returns to the commune to be assigned a job.

A family is not allowed to leave a commune at will. In addition, the commune committee decides what each person's job will be. If a family member is needed elsewhere, the committee will order a transfer. Only through special permission can an individual or a family change jobs or relocate. Therefore, a family's routine changes little and its life to a large extent is planned by the commune.

(44)

OVER A THOUSAND years ago Shanghai was a small fishing village. Today it is the most populated city in the world, with over 10 million people. It is a seaport south of the Yangzi River delta that opens onto the East China Sea. During the second half of the nineteenth century Shanghai was divided into "concessions" by European countries. Their influence can be seen in the different styles of architecture and landscape gardening that remain in certain sections of the city.

Shanghai is now 2,355 square miles and has thousands of commercial and industrial enterprises producing chemicals, paper, electrical machinery, textiles and cars. It is and always has been China's largest port and its principal connection with the outside world. Old Western-looking hotels, office and warehouse buildings stand tall along the waterfront. This is the only city where large billboards advertise clothes, food, radios, watches and cosmetics, all made in China.

We arrive in Shanghai late at night by train from Hangzhou. Immediately we can see and feel that the city is more populated and more cosmopolitan than any of the other cities we have visited.

WE SPEND a special day in Shanghai at one of the city's eleven Children's Palaces. These are centers for extracurricular instruction where seven- to twelve-year-olds go after their regular school classes during the week and on Sundays. They must be recommended by their own schools and have to take an entrance exam.

They learn music, singing, acrobatics and sports, martial arts, magic, drawing, painting, calligraphy, handicrafts, mechanics, dance and ballet.

We visit the Palace at 9:00 on a Sunday morning, and it doesn't seem much different from any other school day in China. At least one

(46)

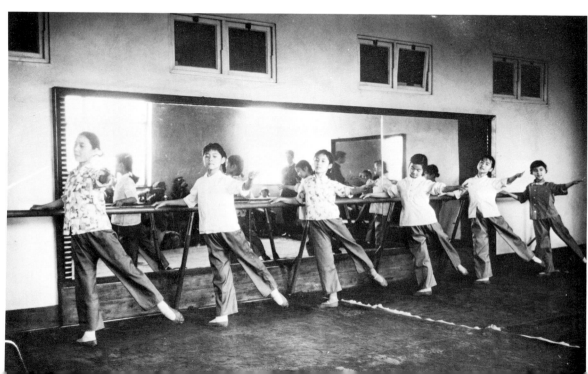

thousand children are at work in the different classrooms. We watch a ballet class of eight- to twelve-year-old girls and one boy, all dressed in blue pants and blouses with red ballet slippers. In a music class, students are in concert playing the violin, xylophone, harp and Chinese string instruments: pi-pa, lute and *qin*. In a drawing class, they use charcoal sticks to sketch a still life of apples and other fruit with care and exactness. In a calligraphy class, firm black brushstrokes move across white rice paper and slowly a geometric character appears. A martial arts class outdoors fascinates us. Once again we are impressed by the dedication, seriousness, and curiosity with which all the children here study and learn.

We play ping-pong with some of the children in their practice room, but they are so skilled that we are no match for them. Outside, Chinese kids try to stand on a skateboard and everybody claps when they stay on.

(48)

(49)

AT THE SHANGHAI Arts and Crafts Research Institute we look at lovely designs and models being created before they are sent to a factory. There are all types of handicrafts: needlework, porcelain, ivory, bamboo, soapstone, dough figurines, paper cutouts, and embroidery.

Paper cutting is really amazing. A man of about fifty-five works rapidly, moving the paper constantly but hardly moving the scissors. In seconds he has cut a sheet of red tissue paper into a complete lace-like dragon.

Streets in downtown Shanghai are livelier and busier than anywhere else we have visited in China. People are everywhere walking, shopping, and eating. We are swept along by the crowds on the sidewalks and in the streets. Jamie isn't even walking; he is pushed straight through the crowds. We are overwhelmed.

People are curious about us here too. As we walk along the Bund—an embankment along the waterfront where Shanghai's modern commercial center is located—they gather around. At first we are embarrassed because we don't know how to react. But they are always gentle and friendly, some just wanting to say hello, and immediately we feel at ease. Ellen, all on her own, is encircled by what seems like hundreds of people. One young girl shyly asks her, "How do you do?"

Later on, shopping in one of the big department stores, we are struck by behavior that is so different from our own customs. As in the streets, people are spitting into metal spittoons, and little kids are allowed to urinate on the floor.

When we get back on the bus, our arms filled with souvenirs for family and friends back home, a crowd once again gathers, and we look out at a sea of people wearing green or blue, colors seen all over the country.

(51)

AT 5:00 A.M. the next morning a few of us get up to film. Being out at dawn and exploring Shanghai's back streets is really great. At first we don't see anybody. But as soon as we start setting up our tripod and movie camera, all kinds of people come out of nowhere to watch us. We move on to another side street and film women burning charcoal in their small stoves for the day's cooking.

(52)

(53)

We feel we have been transported to another era. People are coming out of their front doors and brushing their teeth on the sidewalk. Others are busily cleaning out night-soil pots.

(55)

Now it's 7:00 A.M., and we are in a larger street filming a group of people doing Taiji Quan. They make a great effort to concentrate. It's beautiful to look at them.

(57)

IT IS our last day in China and we feel sad. A stopover in Guangzhou (Canton) before we leave for Hong Kong gives us the feeling that we are no longer in the real China.

Here, people are not dressed as they are in other parts of China. They are wearing much brighter colors in a greater variety of styles. Poverty is much more apparent than in any of the other Chinese cities we visited.

We find it just as unbelievable to think about leaving China as we did about going in the first place. China stared at us and we stared back at the wonders of its people, its sights and its customs.

China is modernizing. We understand why it was important for her to change. We feel she will continue to do so in her own spirit, at her own pace. We made friends in China, and we want to return. But now it is time to leave.

(60)

OUR TRIP to China has come to an end. We are on the plane flying back to New York from Tokyo. A few more hours and China will be in our past.

ZACK: "The friendliness of the people with us. The way they help each other. That was great!"

JAMIE: "The Great Wall was so big and beautiful. Just walking on it. Just seeing it. The Great Wall was China to me."

MONICA: "What I really like is the fact that everybody works. Adults, old people, children, and even little kids in school help with factory work. Everyone has something to do. I like that."

PEGGY: "I was very impressed by the obedience of the kids in school, and even in their homes. They are so attentive and polite. I never saw a teacher or parent get mad at them and I never saw a child crying."

NADIA: "It was fascinating to film in the streets of Shanghai at 5:00 in the morning. The whole city was waking up. People were out on the sidewalks in front of their homes cooking breakfast. Others were brushing their teeth in the streets. I really saw how people live."

JOHN: "I remember very early, at 6:30, one morning visiting the students at People's University next to our hotel in Beijing. They offered us breakfast. They were very curious and asked us all kinds of questions about life in America. One of them asked me, 'Which do you think is better, capitalism or socialism?' I answered, 'I really don't know. I live in a capitalist country. Socialism seems to be working well for you.' "

NAT: "I think of people loading and unloading boats, people pulling heavy cartloads of charcoal, straw, vegetables, grain, wood planks, and bricks, and people building roads with their hands."

ELLEN: "I was walking with Rachel and Jamie on the Bund by the river in Shanghai when all of a sudden I was surrounded by hundreds of Chinese people. There was me, only me, right in the middle with a popsicle in my hand. I was afraid. They were all silent and staring at me. When one of them asked in English, 'How do you do?', I felt better and began talking with them. They had never seen such young Americans before."

DANNY: "At an acrobatic performance in Shanghai the artists of one act came out and cleaned up the stage, or cleared away and set up props for the next show. Every performer stars and cleans. They are taught to work for each other, not only for themselves."

RALPH: "Streets in the city are so busy. People all together eating, cooking, washing, cleaning, relaxing, reading, and sewing, all day long."

KAREN: "My most vivid picture is the huge numbers of little children. They are never by themselves. We saw just as many fathers with their children as we saw mothers with their children. The Chinese say, 'The sky is held up by both sexes.' I saw a young child whose shoelace needed tying ask his teacher to help him. The teacher didn't help him. She told another child to help him."

(62)

RACHEL: "What I really liked was when I was playing a target game, and I kept missing and missing. They didn't say, 'Oh, move on, have the next person go.' Instead, they said, 'Keep trying. You know, have fun. It's to have fun!' They had me trying for a really long time. Finally, they gave me a prize for trying so hard."

MICHAEL: "In the beginning I thought the whole trip was one large shopping expedition. I was overwhelmed. My eyes were shut by what was around me. Somehow they were opened and I saw what China and the purpose of the trip were about. At the Opera School in Nanjing I shook hands with a marvelous old lady and when I looked at her face I saw China, the old and the new. I can't explain why, but I just did."